In this original and beguiling colles her private gallery and guides us throug s not only how works of art have instruc her life became imprinted on the art. A ries, iconoclasts, and infidels (from Marc they, in return, challenge her, "Can you circus act in color, grief-teach yourself / how to dance out the floorboards away from the house into the fields again?" ("Can Cindy Sherman Wear my Hair?"). The art allows for her own reckoning, and with lush language and alluringly reckless syntax, she voices her urgent and vulnerable responses inseparable from the art itself.

MOLLY BENDALL
author of *Watchful*

Drawn into a heady swirl of images riding sinuous syntax, I was curved swiftly, slippery, but unblurred in Elena Karina Byrne's *If this Makes You Nervous*. The poet strokes a verbal impasto with lines that spun me through *kunst*-struck odes to artists here and gone, sudden un-nostalgic memories, "time's own vertigo," and wild eros. Elegiac in mode, not mood, Byrne disinters vision after vision, breakneck and breathless from her "terror-hairless skull," pounding, enveloping, and cutting the lyric into ekphrastic surrender. This is a stunning book.

DOUGLAS KEARNEY
author of *Sho*

Marcel Duchamp, Tony Oursler, Joseph Beuys, and Caravaggio (among others) supercharge Elena Karina Byrne's new book *If This Makes You Nervous*. Wildly fighting the ekphrastic, Byrne's poems get lapel-pulled-close to the dark overtones of being. "Did I mention you are me?" she asks. "I am riddled &/gated, keyed like a car in a future divebar's parking lot." The "bled glitter" and exciting poetics of *If This Makes You Nervous* boils over with memory and meaning. Gorgeous "from the Mona & the Lisa" on.

TERESE SVOBODA
author of *Thatrix: Poetry Plays*

If This Makes You Nervous

If This Makes You Nervous

POEMS

ELENA KARINA BYRNE

OMNIDAWN PUBLISHING
OAKLAND, CALIFORNIA
2021

Cover art by William Wegman, *Untied On Tied Off*, 1973, Silver Gelatin Print
Image courtesy of Marc Selwyn Fine Art

Cover and interior typeface: Adobe Jenson Pro.

Cover and interior design by adam b. bohannon

Library of Congress Cataloging-in-Publication Data

Names: Byrne, Elena Karina, author.
Title: If this makes you nervous : poems / Elena Karina Byrne.
Description: Oakland, California : Omnidawn, 2021. | Summary: "Byrne's
fourth collection of poems offer what she describes as an homage to her
art-immersed upbringing, an ekphrastic weave. The poems challenge
perception as each engages in a visual dialogue between the speaker, her
childhood, society, and 66 artists. The book's lyrical narratives unfold
with psychological urgency and candor, and with linguistic invention as
they re-encounter each artist's unique oeuvre: a balancing act between
beauty and terror, between what is seen and what remains invisible.
Byrne's poems feature the inseparable personal and political, mapping
out emotional, spatial, and gender orientations within the confines of
our visual culture. Her longing and loss color-fields prevail, always
leading the reader in unexpected directions. With grace and galvanic
energy, If This Makes You Nervous is a devotional look into shifting
identity in a preteen's memory, history's collective body as turbulent
mimesis while addressing what is "connected and accounted for" in the
imagination's relativistic measure of time"-- Provided by publisher.
Identifiers: LCCN 2021032501 | ISBN 9781632430953 (paperback)
Subjects: LCGFT: Poetry.
Classification: LCC PS3602.Y76 I3 2021 | DDC 811/.6--dc23
LC record available at https://lccn.loc.gov/2021032501

Published by Omnidawn Publishing, Oakland, California
www.omnidawn.com   (510) 237-5472
10 9 8 7 6 5 4 3 2 1
ISBN: 978-1-63243-095-3

The Inventor of Invented Things opens his eyes, finds himself cradled in the Boy's One Wing.

—KATIE FARRIS

CONTENTS

Rock

Paper

Scissors

Rock

"Everybody expects you to choose rock."

ANDY GOLDSWORTHY'S STICKS & STONES

> *I climb out of my fear.*
> *The mind enters itself, and God the mind,*
> *And one is One, free in the tearing wind.*
> —THEODORE ROETHKE

You are alone. You are alone naked

                        in a forest, surrounded.

Alone, surrounded by a live ossuary of trees, shed twig, spell
of oval stone. You are separate from the forest, in a forest of small
yet perpetuating sounds. No one will hear you breathe. You are
alone, bare hands like large up-curling leaves still soft from the falling.
You shed your expression in the ground next to rounding stone
where the soil is breathing. From grain ends of self-bearing
branches, light mows down on you in the forest, oncoming wind's
near words between its trees' teeth. Spell freefall memory far forward
from your mind to make nothing happen like those nothing spaces between
the rooms you left behind, left alone to be alone, unaccounted for. No one
can hurt you now. Your face, hands, the synonyms of leaves, hair caught
combing a pinecone. Like one pulled potato, a child here
alone, falling out of your house made from cut down trees...

before the squall hit,

before five-bodies' weight in boulders thrown from
the breakwater. We stood at the window. We lay calm on wood-colored
beaches. Dreams don't sink children with the ship. Ships carrying other
languages are found empty atop mountains in far countries. After giving
directions, I watched the woman, crossing our street, hit by a car the color
of dusk and she sank

at once, as if into a hole. I carried
that hole in my stomach for years. A sinkhole, also known as swallow hole,
a doline caused by some depression, by some form of ground collapse. In
the '60s TV was filled with them. On islands as quicksand & as men's
mouths, immolation fire's cadmium-midst of protest. Films of ditches, war
holes, numberless graves unaccounted for. Running

before a storm's roiling, I
learned to jump wide spaces, roof to roof. I believed the wet
black head of a horse breathed desert clouds over my sleeping body.
A child can be anyone. Where sea waves can look like blown wheat
leveled by wind. At her end of the day, the long walk

wilderness rest of her life.

WHICH WAR IS THIS, LAURIE ANDERSON?
—Hurricane Sandy

Knit-heavy clouds darning. Haven't we earned *the right* to combat,
earned *Heart of a Dog* knowing home? This live river, splitting its
blackened stitch, gives up uncut gemstones while crossing
streets, highway, over Central Park's grass. The hurricane's downed
daylight overhead, a Hoag's Cloud felt now like one farmer's
thousand-year field plowed open as the mouth of another
child shot *in our new town*, new country's Cigar Galaxy that
the naked eye can't see, not meant to be smoked past making
stars. Also called M82 like those red thumb-sized bombs
my brother & friends placed in storm drains beneath our houses
so many M80 spring sewers ago, waking dusk into believing it
was dawn. Now water, *freak water* raises moon's dead river
into bled glitter instead of road where just as injustice as
a match lit in the mouth, as this city drowning within its
own arms. What time is it if you can't hear it coming, carrying
horizon's cow carcass, imagination's house air-size
unclear & what star's thrown dice like pulled teeth from your
head will it be? Which war-making of ourselves to see only storm?

TURNER, STRAPPED TO THE MAST:
—1969

Winds'
                thrown snow hives, splitting the sea's white lips, were heard
that same year my pre-teen body's biremes sank & rose with the gales.
The terminal roar seemed a whole planet's belly width, one pressed
heel of the heaven's open palm. We saw the painted floor-to-ceiling
stained-glass window's paneled scene sealed to the staircase's top
landing... whoever got there first: a new child game. So, from one iron
banister's black bottom curve, friends ran & hurtled in fierce competition,
stopping at its edge. This would be my first year's storm water hitting
in the face—the Turner year Father teaches me how to draw like his
students facing a kneeling knight in pose: know, you have to put
the armor on. It's the only vantage point danger: mortality equals, at once,
hunger for & defiance. But like the Romans who filled their Colosseum
with a mock sea, ships & battles to please the Emperor, my friend had
one thought only: to win & doublehand the church-colored glass. Then,
the outside buckled back into the window's one collapsing lung: fallen
storm shards of winged color, its nature's wrath-afterlife

                                                    at our feet.

AWOL ERIZKU'S RESCUED HIGH CACTUS

I am   certain came from the sore-same desert they body-dragged

my cousin Mark into   so as to long torture him for testifying against
the released drug dealer he fell from   Desert flowers & ready rain's
flung spring curtain on the ground mixed with blood   No police   no
police protection   & no pretty-cut picture to a dry sky that also won't
care about his childhood or abandoned cars   another fallen body foiled
rotting as food for animal   His flowers' hallucinatory color sprouting
is full wheel away from *Duchamp Detox Clinics*   now courtesy of the
artist   This room   my room   re-imagines his hour taken from all hours
I know I heard him scream white   woke loud into full silence & wondered
what was real   or where the tree fell & how many times it did fall before
he was heard. Humans   a *force of nature* no matter what anyone stops

to tell you   Force from nature   Greening is grief too   you   times two

RACHEL WHITEREAD: IT'S SO

I was always like an old child
—CHANTEL AKERMAN

You could almost lick   those sugar cubes stacked in sleep
find   the hexahedron ark floating today's ocean missing
its human animal leaving   home   Grief is an impression
of a missing table under the table   a body departed   withdrawn
from the body floating   the color of Halloween candy
wrappers. I lived   a whole afternoon under the leftover
house boards in our dying garden after my one sister
died   Half-sister   half death of my thinking   about death
at nine   A black hole can be measured   by the sheer speed of
what is orbiting around it   If you withdraw   one object from
its space in a room   measure   what's left   all the empty parts
you have a child inside a box   A box thinking   outside itself

No, no one
gets to be happy here unless happy means *Pain
is exquisite*. Follow us to the animal bedroom, all the way to
the drive-through chapel & walkabout child fairytale day
hour it takes to become a stranger, where you can't see
you, your hand on the heart like a small anvil. Where mothers
will make mistakes politicians appear speaking from sea-trash
& border wire's mounting, meshed lingo. There will be a money jar,
pink hot water bottle, one duck-handle umbrella gun waiting for
you. What fathers take can make gunpowder-snuff for the blind. But
come. Come here anyway to this continent in a floating wardrobe
boat. Follow the past to missing solitude. This is where you will
weep from your eyes only, making no sound, as if, all along, your
voice voyaged away from cage, far, from your body.

ANDREI TARKOVSKY:
RECKONING THE WATER RAFT
—*April 4, 2020*

Now I focus on cold questions where I can't get up from this weight gurney
of a bed, where *I'm about to employ to close the window* here, as self-harm

creates a planet. To prefer the curse of self-harm with no timeframe—why
I follow nature's algorithm of loss & constantly moving light in this film.

A man on pause enters my interlude before sleep, floats on a low moss raft
where I must be made of water. Water is its own audience. How *It suffers*

rhythmically, to and from… Look, light always breaks my skin there:
One cloud's shearling seen passing on its wool, a pennyweight ahead of

this estuary's dead-end ocean. One radio drowning in its own metal voice
can be heard. One billystick pile of tree debris. Wooden tub eels in a tangle

take his consciousness out for a walk. *They all have, like me, their*
future in the past, but I'd have to be a man to possess our kiss, one boot

on fire left home. Psychology of black railroad ties across the grass cliff's
drop-off. To come with sackcloth silence still meddling with me. I'd have

to keep some equivalent violence, small corpses of insects left brackish-
behind. Between sinking telephone poles, a scarecrow in his black suit

broods like memory. Off his back, I'll wear the same brother coat
nailed down beside him—& over his shadow's broken-away bird.

HANNAH HÖCH COLLAGE:
EVERYTHING ME WAS UNMOORED OBJECT,

left on my own insides too long like her *brushflurlet* heads, my own tilted in
a scene-sunless garden, endangered: part capture & cut against latest Hitler & his
ongoing. I am ahead of myself: He of she, she of she, having it her animal
way, naked & in for Dada's *Die Puppen* & dandy there in the dulcet angst I feel being
a boy-girl in puberty, belly down to the sky helm, on a full-run earthward,
playing till dark wakes around me. From one dog call after sliding the fence's far
side of our neighbor's frown & for sore tongue in its toil, I am riddled &
gated, keyed like a car in a future dive bar's parking lot. My jean studs catch ice
plant's green slime. It's hurt beauty worth no dowry to the past. It's fear's
invitation riding one hobbyhorse hereabouts close to home where my best friend's
father shouts above his flattop haircut, early '70s rage-red-face for it, for end
of his *gook war,* finding another whiskey kick out back, lips, large as handlebars.

Losing measure in the face tearing apart, my skinny bones, pent breath, my bike
thrown down to the grass as I see them running game against all direction...

it is rather the form of the impossibility of fleeing.
—CATHERINE MALABOU

You like to drink
water from the neighbor's army-green hose
because it still smells like summer hitting the hot ground. Here,
you are one age, long before you can be at all woman,
ripped wind, statistic. Before dusk's late curfew
sleepover or simply because Mom was pill-happy home with
Dad, you boot-break her oval makeup mirror without anger, scatter its new
scant face shapes into the far yard earth between a petting zoo of plants
that needed to see sky's fresh violence . . . dirt-colored hair stuck to your
cheek. From the *d'Avignon* room of one
spectator, Mom tried, for her sake, not yours, to stop your bad side
that seemed unstoppable, an inebriated sea breaking itself apart, the form
of you, unrecognizable & disappearing over & over into summer's
darkening olivine body of sand . . . Mother
was always staring at her beautiful facein mirrors, as if it
might change.
Her rear-view one, half-cocked
back at her while driving, terrified me. Faces slowed or sped by us: back
of a redhead, an apple's half facing forward, floating baby nose, eyes
aligned with ears, or only sunglasses like twin poker cards, turned.
Picasso knew so well what he had in front of him: women neither
affirmed or denied belonging. That's why his painting could destroy them.
I really didn't know which Mother face was reflected in the windshield
ahead, which bottle-blue eye was open on the moving road.

CLONING DUCHAMP IS MATHEMATICS

—for Brendan Constantine

or "pataphysics," is addition

in the open playpen of gray matter & is giving up
your ghost chessboard. Bicycle wheels hang from the trees . . . *heat is visible,*
a floating bruise over the garden. Two of everything me is there in a room-
less room, my adult rearview stalker & mother's face, mine, never
asked for. After all,

Mother's fear labored her life mimicking my toy Slinky ribs' accordion-
countdown to each stair. I'm the one girl in the unseasonably warm car
about to be stolen, first ever to lose all my blood in the wrong backyard,
as twelve ladders stack themselves between a neighbor's oil sweat & bonfire
& my body. To breach the split season with colds. Favor the evil ice cream
man in his singing truck that slowly rocks down our street, its tinkering
bells suffering on your behalf. I make no sense to

myself. My head won't vesper bitter, mend straight lines because I worry
too much that I've hurt someone's feelings, opened the umbrella inside
the closet one too many times: it prefers to be upside down, a lizard's
hammock in the desert with a witch-way industry of free tumbling from
the black boot-jaw-lock on

this noir wind.

in *Caricature, Hard Case* yelling from under a floral
couch thrown from the 50's. So very freak of nature we are when
disturbed, haunted like his camera obscura, all aperture & apparatus
of language left behind: *you can never get the rain to come down
when you want it to,* never keep the mind

> from doubt, rubber shoes from squeaking. I can hear
> drought's bark beetles ticking & ticking, that thrown
> voice, my own, & each cloth-stuffed dummy's half

sleeping face. Elvis & his twelve-gauge points right at the television till
all else is child's play, the skin allied to chaos & onion memory: I'd mime
crying just to scare the dark back into the cedar cupboard
since no one confuses their own fear for something else. Oursler's no
dummy hiding in the corner. This family topology might as well
include mother's color feathers over rhinoceros skin. To live in
the chamber population of Moebius riddle-dolls is all caption
daemons caught by the latest War. Never allow your animals.
Never your animals to be shown in someone's traveling circus tent

> the color of sea candy.

WILLIAM WEGMAN'S WEIMARANER WILLIAM

—be a stand-in

Two shoes   I took off at the party & left them in a *footfield* with others

by the door   looking back at them ditched   looking at

                              their Weimaraner-brown obedient mouths
I wondered if they

revealed personality   could be identified as belonging to me   W.W.

photographed his shoes once   old pair   *Untied on, Tied off,* 1973

they, together   I only remember because I thought I

once recognized their sockless near twins in

Van Gogh's painting   just

                                        askew   worn-in as if far

windows wept away from them   as if

once   gray animals in our clothes groaned   then slept   Children

love or hate shoes   as they do dogs   teach them-

                                        selves how to tie them up   keeping

left & right side by side   well-behaved

by the bed   Psychologists say that

we choose pets & colors for a reason   We look alike   So   Be Other

I say   Be a stand-in once *Souvenir*   *Leggy*   *For A Moment*

while collapsing   *Into The Ocean*   room

BEFORE THE COCK CROWS
MEMENTO MORI: CARAVAGGIO

—Mother

Tormentors inviting you into this: His   exile light underpainting devotion
saw nocturnal-lavish-animal coming to a death banquet. You   were caught
by surprise of your own voice, smell of her   mater skin filling the room
half-eaten by the sound of the nurse's television merry. These age paintings
debate much more capture accurate than puts me here: circa 1620, 2010,
then & then. Caravaggio left everything to gesture, feelings to befall. She's
on the brink, sees ahead of what you want to say.   Did I mention you are me?
I mirror. Opulent the costume to keep from thought's intruder, scholar who
knows better. You are invited here to be voyeur. The unanimous black
background, the format barely contains all of us hymning this pause,
the pang. That's the force of it, where everything between past & future
happens. Ask her, but you can't, so you both window-stare at the outside's
level image unreachable. I've never blood-let or pig's feet from a jar, never
abused an orphan pear into thinking bruise-rot   then earth-owned
without a second bite first.   She taught that.

As if ambiguity's onsite workload whistle
in the act of climax breathing like oars
the cold slickwater back. Breathing
over the skin, caught staring, starting in on
long enough to know this: no street creed
asphalt & fault into final dirt, no male
As if this country's added lack of empathy
already add up to my funeral of nail
peel & violent laughter's perfume bottles
where one quarter horse half-sleeps in his
limits of grief can't be stopped or looked
in the eye: Why I'm no one's fallen apple
rind-green dress. I forget how to see the
moon declaring my ex-husband's dirty
I'm over an overkill silence. The sex
into a still-life void, another woman's face
Nobody's business that *their features are*
my horse's body now, *made up of water,*
wash having no single declaration
left to drain. This might yet have me
trapped in parsimony & still pleading

caught us
dragging
an orchard
the face just
corner divides
from female.
hours didn't
clippers, police
left bedside
musk—these
at for long
wearing her
oil-unwashed
water tale.
minutes turn
at a price.
sleeping inside
oiled bath
expression
here, *laid bare,*
for fruit.

DALÍ'S GLUTTON RECIPE DEAD: POLITICS

Rest assured that for each member you will pull off he will scream so that he will be eaten live rather than dead.

Nearly asleep in sweet trifling she lay out alone on this NYC lawn, raw dirty pigeons skirting a circle edge's raked flame of leaves. Who walks past her served-up bathing body with burgundy sun on the way to work doesn't see the fountain's web-footed waters, its spring horses flash & stir, its escape of water, loose silver chains spit breaking onto the concrete. Didn't see the corn flour cakes walking to school, the jellied cod or siren shoulder. *Pierced heart & Prawnparfait* daily hurry on their way, their way. *Le Chat flanqué* de Rats from these streets cut chatter for another's scent, pass salt under their tails. How many Guineafowl for a murder, pig skin, headless eels peppered on bread today? Before night's rolling-pin arrives, before cicadas start their singing-out the heat, he drops feet from her, a Peregrine & his pigeon flesh strips of bacon, carrots & onion soaked in cherries. She pays no notice, her little bits of butter clarified swimsuit orange peel & roe set onto the middle sour grass since all sounds of the fountain are salpicon. We the people, we *ought to transform the art of eating into an olographic ecstasy!*

FRITZ KAHN'S MACHINE BODY SURVIVES 2018 IN A SARCOPHAGUS

> *Surround yourself with beauty, for ugly comes on its own*
> —FRITZ KAHN

Don't ask. Whose center of gravity sends an acrobat four black wheels

every two political minutes apart to make symmetry happen on its own
accord... A chord of spilled blood, *das wunder* plasma pulling from

center to winter's spent center. Don't, it says. There are new mixed

species stacking people & new animals my size with better brains I bet.
See it in the heart moving an elevator up, window oar-frame, an all-

response to time, life that claims our one obsession: to be alive, to live

its dirty fruit windfall. The double soul, earth & egg, sends us far from
home through the mind's seawater thunder to ring the doorbell more

than once. Now take that new Supreme Court Judge, his industrial pipes,

error apparatus itch, defense mechanism's pyrogens' fever to kill before
being killed, fearing for harm, the drunken whaler's man-handle going.

STYLE OF IMPRISONMENT: DIANE ARBUS
PREDICTED THIS VIRUS

this scrutiny has to do with not evading facts
—DIANE ARBUS

She worked her way into the winter's dyad sideshow

of homeless tents & full metal shopping carts tipping their
amidship cloth sails. To the next passerby wearing my same
shirt, I said, go & goad the drunkalogue, be dissonance
like dropping your unbelted pants at the movies. An act
of betrayal will get you an ignored corpse in the creek's
icebox scene, smiling for no reason. Since I couldn't
be dead honest with myself between rooms. Since
Words themselves act as deeds, unwilling to break
bread for bird song. The paradox skin still shines in this
same direction. But hard-wired we are after the warfare
referendum before Venus de Milo held her river hair sex-
down, an outcast of blown-on beauty I once saw in
the cruelty of schoolgirls against girls. How shells
& coffee grounds share a planter's home soil—
bodies' flux asphyxia-suffering. For instance. For
instance. For *stakes of blame,* the last photograph you saw
shows a suicide shrug, shoulders bare & a virus blur in both
eyes. Even Jane Mansfield's hair bow & my doctor's Venice
bird mask hung for one cousin plague are not alone. It's her
best shot at showing freaks alike where nature mirrors

our bathroom life & sets fire to itself in the heat.

For:

　　　　three in-days, animal America | tore at the felt blankets
surrounding him. At an ambulance distance, race hate, war |
hours, & team white-out | police: we were all brought in to see
the artist, shepherd, the shaman in time's split prison-grey divide,
sharing tooth & nail | desire to conquer himself like one common
tied nightmare | dredged up from a waking summer swamp, to
bob the head to nod, prodded. What chaos from freedom | came
oscillating animal rhythmed cycles. I saw gold straw like cut coyote |
fur in the male | corner, those 50 *Wall Street Journals* | peed on, I saw
my brother standing on his bed in the next room home, not knowing
where he belonged. I heard the pealed night call, his fear-run | down
the stairs to open our front door. But no | one would be there, no one
with that taut *desire to heal*, no offstage | cane that would find his

　　　　　　　　　　　　　　　　　　　　　　　　　　neck.

AT AGE 6, MARINA ABROMOVIĆ BEGAN LIVING WITH HER PARENTS

and I, wanting
a live white mouse, not a false rabbit fur one hung by its tail from
the pet store to be dragged by our cat's claws in a double death ritual
across our carpet, began wearing boy clothes, digging yard dirt with
a severed doll head, cut my pants on wire & climbed between backyard
teeth of broken fences, crashed my bicycle for brother's friends, shoved
the fist, full laughing, into my mouth... You can enjoy replay and *you can
push your body to do things*, creating one bellow-blown burst of light in
the brain: biting your lip blue to feel the heart pulse down to its left wrist,
pulling back the black scab from the knee to watch it bleed again. Pain
is relative to need until the performance ends. Push as much air into your
lungs as you can when someone else hurts another in front of you: watch it
unfold, extricated: Right there, people being hurt by other people long before
we betrayed memory, bodies in final exhale from a kerf-overlap of sounds,
human weapons filling these animal hours without limit.

FRANCIS BACON SWALLOWS THE HEAD WHOLE,

—Lynne

face, eye to tongue, into car's cry failing down this motion-going   rain's
befuddling her still-life body, its burial ground against current   wash, its
ask-open-orifice slipping for   water face without shape, a long slide into
mud of one color, now no sex for car's final violence, silenced acre of
oxygen forced from the torqued trees falling with her & torn sheet metal.
All head's the head ajar, twisted, crowning at ravine bottom, unruly
time lost in this upended night scour turn of events, religious as Hopkins'
groans grinds language in her last *thoughts*, now, passed on as our private
thoughts, swallowed head-whole with a pillow   boiling over in its memory,
quick-sliding slur-back into carapace's collapsing gabion cage where   rain is
 paint purifying in a sudden tantrum, *remaking appearance* in death's tantric
pace with her naked   swimming limbs' spiritless bulk, a catch for leaves, this
new impasse, her soft brain now a coughed-up owl pellet of fur, her one week lost
face raised from   water's pursed grey lips & voice's hebenon long down   river…

PIERRE HUYGHE'S CRAB WORE MY SLEEPING MASK

from behind
        its *post-humanist* lifeworld   beneath the public Palais
de Tokyo   its underwater red rock-range depth contains this calendar's
standstill   where water & air are limb-alike   Crab
carries her eyeless Brancusi muse face   her borrowed house   slowly
Its expression never changes like my neighbor's small boy
                              revived after drowning.
Dusklight entity.   Pierre's crab
carries its *cognitive map* in my direction to tell me we are free
from dying: a sound of swarming bees rose seaweed-
above one beached whale missing her wind instrument.   Fish
appear with beer can holder necklace rings & sea turtles mistake
adrift color plastics for food   those parts of us thrown
into buried water without constraint   taint on the salt
                                  tongue.   Death

is your child no longer conscious of who you are   is the pool
water   guise of a mother's handed down crystal
necklace   breaking over his skin.   The sleeping muse
welcomes not waking   She faces the fisherman's glassed-
in sky never weighed down   or measured
by bottom-bearing bleached reef beds   equal to any
consolation harm.

Paper

"Rock is way too obvious, and scissors beats paper."

IF CONTENTS IN / JOSEPH CORNELL'S BOX

                                        I won't give way
to false teeth left in a champagne glass after a fight
nor fall from the shadow box into the boxer's black gloves
smoke your pipe in the tortoise north darkness
                                     between stars
deranged on the moon's *Geographique* map of your face rising like
one scrap planet   one startled bluing childhood doll head that calls for
recriminating light   Cassiopeia's soul over another lover's bent knee
I can't find a contagion of wanderlust   the plumage-distance in a red
bird's body   now aviary-flown because we knew how long it would
take an apothecary's colors to come bottling home
                                  You underestimate
me   my family's inheritance of feeling   its open airless universe &
you pay the color white a visit   you   startled   deadout-you   collecting
keys & coin   are afflicted by newsprint flesh   waiting for stacks of
matches to strike light under the skirt's twirl & heat's abyss
                         I can't for this, be contained!

LYNDA BENGLIS, WE'RE COOKED IN LA,

in memory of artist Robert Chuey

confusing ourselves on impulse to completely melt-down together like that heat-
welt of hundred crayons left in the childhood driveway, whether we,
now or not, like it, to "look at this and just die"

ahead of ourselves, suffocate under Lynda's *Eat Meat* giant bronze,
or inside my cousin's carpet once he rolled me off the bed to a hard landing
where I couldn't flee or breathe. Far from her beeswax hive, we will take
a resin course of action, turn & gut-twist to be fluid, fall to our lover's floor
without form, be continuous. Or pour ourselves from a great height, whole,
into a glass held out by another's hand

because we want to trust. Yet like history, look how objects fail us by
default, by means. I'd make all my mistakes visible, add her Day-Glo pink
to see my own blood clot, bring back those who are gone, change that
corner traffic light that phrased a drunkard's truck clear through his front
windshield, turning its glass to snow & an active noun, set down. Because
any idea of his painting is incomplete, bile-black at best, now. Because live

long enough here & you will see Tar Pits boil over these sidewalk seams,
freezing like my dog's lawn excrement, mat in color, holding memory of
the previous self & heated to gleaming.

WHY ALL PORTRAITS ARE A FORM OF TAXIDERMY, RICARDO NICOLAYEVSKY

She should have been part his, a selfhood LA film still:
limb's memory-inoculum & reckless too, passing her own
oneiric face through the school halls: to answer to no one,
endanger the time alone. City is conurbation,
                    a merge. Look, she's one unworthy
                    eye for seeing white pull out, for dancing the reverse
into a square-cut field's blurred frame to frame.
That could be anywhere, but I tell you it's not just
                    anyone. She has since been set free to be the predicate of
a sentence where fields come into view & come up as a friend's lost
soundtrack. Elegy is alive, not well, stripped of its wet clothes, pool-floating
face-down, wrapped rubber tubing & a peeled light-swatch like a leaf
                    stain's negative image on the sidewalk ahead. How do you
                    become your own portrait? A film camera holds still
for those who are moving. It was always hard for her
to hold still as a child. She could not help herself. Teachers
                    wanted to punish her, hovered into view, wood ruler held
                    high up above the head, measuring their own voices. I bet
they saw a four-legged chicken, not child. Doubling on anatomy.
She refused to hear them, felt only moving air's constant surrender.

WHERE IS DEAD ARTIST JACK GOLDSTEIN?

The mother has locked the yellow bathroom door to protect her
child from the father. California trees everywhere, at all heights,
unaccounted for. A foreground from which to climb, to escape,
where the one purple dark will be made. Where lightning strikes
before a horizon & a building is caught. Where cut grass keeps its
intractable position all the way to the adult artist asking Mother
about our caged Minah bird. Drugged, in slow motion, he's smiling
indigo's heel of black. In his films: the far white door slams over &
over just before a man, running, gets there, the MGM lion roars, roars.
One light bulb flickers in the grassdark, with his heartbeat six feet above
ground, above the buried man, him, listening, a bare pipe from which
to speak down like the ear canal of God. Jack's name is repeated over
& over, out loud. This intimate interaction repeats, repeats all night.
His chosen center of earth is unaccounted for. Jack, I knew, when I was
a purple child, right before I was one adult when he stopped making
films, when he painted canvases much larger than deceit, than our
bathrooms holding the welt-split light. Where bathrooms at home were
not closed coffins from which to hear the outside world speak your name.

CAITLIN BERRIGAN'S TRANSFER CULTURAL DESPAIR-WEAR

-—beyond the framework of the human.

I would colony in | clear plastic there with her, appetite the inhuman

fight to keep salt away from those snails crossing my | pillowcases.
There's a case for short term violence, power & lit | desire away from
commerce capital in an empty building that wakes with live | things
at night in another country you care for. There's a | narrative of you
in an unfinished state of address. Take it, take it somewhere new.
Know this brink of living starts. | Shit & marshmallows belong in
the same imagination place, just as adults & children deploy a rung-
unfinished view from above. We are bound for palimpsest, successive
drowning of our | emotions based on the day's map-making over every
memory | ocean. Checklist your evacuation plan. Deep time moves here:
mineral |vegetable from the ground, animal from air | a volcano's
ash-cloud is your mind hovering planet earth. *The* | *rage was there before*

you. It will remain after, as | happy will leave its | oil-slick on the water.

REALITY MAY STILL BE UNACCEPTABLE GERHARDT RICHTER: A REPEATING DREAM I'M BELLY-DOWN AT ELEVEN

beneath barbwire
                    like bedsprings during night-climbs   wet crop dirt under
my shirt   saving babies in the dark slide of building's vents into canvas
flap backs of trucks   a chaos of fleeing.   Tell me, isn't that art?

An in-crisis or crime-pull toward & away from. Color block   lines
moving toward & away: painting is a leavetaking.   *Death is
a leavetaking.*   Fleeing, great grandfather   out of fear   changed his
name with his family's country   confounded something that is still
missing there where I see a truck that fell from the eroded cliff before
I was born   an indivisible ocean &   hill   bitten by cactus needles
fennel weed like language in an unbroken string-cruelty of color   too far
away to see   yet look at all disquiet-pictures that fall into our laps   *Three*

times the head of the dead   daily coming blur-back out of history's chaos
like hairpins falling from pine trees   or dried blood hemming the floor
edge of your bedroom's closed door   the same child's tongue-color of
                                                            final rust.

scared the carbon hell out of cracked colors, clouded & crowded.
Mike drove those stuffed animals out of their bored silence off
the wall into my terror-hairless skull. He said, he said. Into social
media box frame, all USA Mike hurt the forest of small shiny things
like sweet fizzed chaos of thinking for me. Kelley, pallor-drug-boy-
toy, underground dummy culture breathing a clustering crack-cartoon-
swoon-song centered, really a knock on someone's haven halo, he was.
For bedstead master, Nazi cock flag flown, for sleepless crosswalk brief
encounters, he, he, sticky. I looked & looked for the world of my own
feeling faces, born away from fear: Not a bad one-eyed child of our country
cozying up to uncontrolled complex candylands you carry around, junkyard
empire politics choking you with a dull home spoon so you can pretend he
sees his own headshot backfiring its last unstitched expression, your blameless
Mom & Dad in the big Mike Kelley room watching you watch too.

THE HAT WE CANNOT PUT ON IS FULL OF HONEY: ANN HAMILTON

I

She's trapped in the chair, knits her hands in amber honey. Hear
       the sticky sounds, imbricate lapping from the hat in her lap.
       The heat's swept floorboards are hammered down. Down comes
       a mother, unable to sleep with a bees' soufflé mess, minor
       scuffles, waggle & a father in his own fisticuffs.

II

Pennies count themselves indefinitely where you can hear your
       teeth grinding & sheep calling from another country. Commerce
       counts as the head becomes one tumbleweed uprooted
       from its sagebrush hillside. Now, then. Tell me, who's made
       for the human clade, descendent music measure inside the chest?

III

So many cast wax votive heads fief together in one glass coffin's
       attic vitrine, her confine for language. No daughter comes to
       know the unmatching mother & father this way. Carrier pigeon.
       Caper vine. Crepuscular. Landscape-driven, I'm word-trapped in her
       chair, at a nosebleed height, & it's a private matter.

NO SUSPENDING BRUCE NAUMAN

—M Ampere (1973)

who would never be woman. Never a *madame.* Never

　　　　　　　　　　　　　　　　　　　　a chair. Never

woman

　　　　in a hoar chair sitting. An empty wood chair

　　　　　　　　　　falling, forgetting its color like sky. Of

man. A language. A hostile imperative. Ugly command-mouth. No. Double

backward-words, never. *Doppel-gänger*

　　　　　　　　　　in for it.

　　　　　　　　　　Slowing speed of all

things except the genderless brain tethered to the body.

　　　　　　　　　　In for going. Never Nauman as

fate of an anonymous woman.

　　　　　　　　　　He-suspended-word. She, above herself,

limbs of a chair.

　　　　　　　　　　Are ugly nameless objects they are. They doubled in

the M. She never of him.

　　　　　　　　　　His thinking from the seat. Seat of the matter art. The split

　　　　　　　　　　horizon, nowhere to

be seen from the current elected body of officials.

　　　　　　　　　　Chair lifted, attempting altitude,

to be empty as your thought, as nonsensical language startling her face

　　　　　　　　　　　　　　　　　　into one

feeling. Never

be any weather-chair of a woman with arms & legs, facing one direction. Horizonal. Vertical. Compound noun compounded by the
fate of them. No.
Never
just Nauman there. Here. Now we are.
No, never. Watch as you read.
An age-old question stands: language-matter
to be read in a mirror:
MAMPERE/RAPEME.

No *double* gets up. A *walker* walks.

INSTEAD, THE HEAD: LORNA SIMPSON

Instead   the head is turned away, obscured, the head is turned on by
a winter bonfire flowers rising from the top of the head like
memory from hair's bird-auction knitted between dusk & dawn.

Instead   one eye's opened ashtray, or both obscured, follow in pattern
filigree-knit dark, like language on the skin that like them, *won't
take no for an answer,* won't wear you out, won't stick the chicken

        wishbone in the throat before sleeping. But who will witness
an error in these repetitions, in all circles as you fall square, feel your
body parts, *feel the ground sliding from under you* like the very last part
of your photo skin wishing itself forward & away, its last text turned
film-back through US history's hate still smelling like your burnt hair of
chip cookies & baby milk.

Instead   your body viewed from behind, forever breaking
its invisible silken butterfly on the collarbone's only wheel.

—there is no gray area

I. WHEREAS UNCOLORED

into engaging the first coaxed gray
area: Panel believes in findings, in front of a grey door,
the verbally sinking bed was about erratic bodies in violation
& ash to other *grey* occasions before sex had sex.

II. WHEREAS ACHROMATIC

between lock penis and voice
across the naked apartment, once the kisses & of touches, tinkling
keys hymn across the room, both parties explained. In the past,
facts violate Offense Number 5, (kisses and touching) and
Respondent on the other side of Complainant, moved—to the other
side of tattoo, believed or coerced, bleached of color, given
the frequency of engagement.

III. WHEREAS OPAQUE

expresses hoof agreement with these naked
beliefs, the gray matter, the foundation of their relationship was based—
likely immediate in the spilled days & weeks they were at length, routinely.
Stationary bodies violent, kink, and erratic alone. Disaffect the personal.
Who does hide everywhere, who does partner feared otherwise & we said
so, in wilting grey. Only. They, they Panel completion.

IT'S TIME DAMIEN HIRST DIED IN THE PILL BOX,

in the hurt love of God, in the shark tank-same place you
put yourself in danger, in secret, in the butterfly wing's solace
ripped from blue flight, motor-driven, paint-splattered loophole
dial to the child you were. It's a shit-hour sense of consciousness
seal broken & monstrous world access-easy located on the dot.
See it? Crossing the crosswalk, doing his Leonardo thing, that
theater life-drawing from which you take a stuffed animal in
the dark act out into the open again. A piano must fall on you.
What else is there to death & art-hymn of the body you hate?
A new arrangement of diamonds in the skinned skull sees fit to
call, as glittering is seeming & seething... Words teeming
between your teeth where you can't breathe, where you'll live
medicine-forever in the darkened blue bygones of extinction like
this: suspended, your relic head upright as your reputation.

FIRING SQUAD, CONVERGENCE, JACKSON POLLOCK

See: Father's art school

smells like the afterlife of charcoal.
                                    The art room floor, war-littered with every color,

what babies make spit-shouting from highchairs, juice, food escaping
toothless loose mouths & fat hands that, over time's absence, beat
                                        the solid air to music only they hear.

What are days called we first learn to walk, singing, the others

taken from us at deaf checkpoint by strangers? I'm always
caught barefoot,

something of Mother's paintbrushes in my hair, Dad's large hands
holding open the white door as if it were an easel. Ex-

                    husband wants to tell me to put on shoes,

that I might get hurt by what I cannot see.
Yet, I stand in this one spot, eyes closed, still,
to listen & guess at flight, face all the birds spilling

out, overlapping the garden's excess entropy. They are my
only evidence

                    I cannot plan what might happen now
                                        holding my tongue.

TO BE SEEN: HOWARDENA PINDELL
SEES WHAT REMAINS

ongoing, in motion like yard children, clad men skating,
unclad diving, like thought-action, hands to air drawn

arrows to numbers, the race trace & accident studies of

her fallen punch holes, chads' color fields overlaid,
not the color of children-bones, a roster of them,

a recount, clean screenshot sheet. In what fractured feel
of debris work could I find teeth grinding down in the garden,

dial back to my friend hiding in my closet for three days until

leaping, all *glitter, talcum powder and perfume,*
a twelve-year-old's two-story fall to flee

from her father & postcard trade-in on the past? Circled

& squared there, I slide ice over the double heat of
my lips not to speak of it, but I can see her still

breathing under my heaved pile of clothes. Pindell
frees this canvas from the frame, controls the chaos.

Pindell circles in on the question.

My friend was hungry for sweets, only in secret.
I fed her only in the middle dark.

found our underearth with the double palm's fruit-curve of his head
held just inches from the hospice pillow, or so I imagined,
$$\text{\& his feet,}$$
a walk away from me in their new whitened skin, already cold marbled
perfection fish. But to be changeless is insatiable, implied by
$$\text{the next}$$
move. Who said we can't bring back the dead? Daphine's hands in
this tree already swung light shards into a passing falcon's eye.
$$\text{Pluto's hand}$$
is still hard-pressed into Proserpina's bare ass down in a closed
basement like an adult's childhood confused by blood-middle of this city.
$$\text{But artist}$$
Gian Lorenzo executed father's tenderness, his love for something once
understood: brain speed of a horse before it races: artist in his bloom classroom
$$\text{seat leaping off}$$
suspension bridge of a page: what's always unfinished as the mouth opens
its voweled dark to final dark ahead of it. Whatever ecstasy says of you,
$$\text{it's loud and alive.}$$

All planetary oranges fall from the grove like his stopped heart before
Santa Ana winds turn it burning ash &, sooner or later, no longer to you,
$$\text{belongs.}$$

JESSICA GRINDSTAFF BROUGHT BACK
THIS PHANTOM LIMB

found   after the Fukushima Daiichi nuclear disaster, its shoulder pain

felt   on the shoulder of an unyielding highways' shouldering death's one

wave   in the 2011 ocean shoal groan-heaving headlong to Honshu shore.

For   I cannot be seen without it. For it hurts without brain's conversation.

It   glows green in the dark while sleeping like a new sea animal found in

inebriated   unreachable depths where mother-descent means any direction,

where   volcanic vents breathe only exhale. Its hand hurts especially when

reaching   for my face now. It was how I knew I would not forget myself all

those   times I couldn't see, couldn't recognize a feature aged overnight in

that   sleep theater of surprise where glacier ice air is always empathy-clean,

forcing   the past to feel like a survivor's story. We snowballed, became limb

puppets   & survived the family drowning wave after wave. But fallout is our

haunted   house in phantom fields that live inside you as the furniture collapses

back   to groundwater & is replaced with doll parts too small to belong to me.

told us Hollywood was a verb on the painted stretcher   fretting,
we knew it was true. There, I am *LIGHTLY DISTURBED*   standing
under his window, he's so damned handsome in the version   extreme
& in-betweens where unlikely color thinks itself from the page.   Sex
drive-in movie theater screen seen. No sound box to clip on.   Say-over
a succession in the language-place, body-place. Language   eventually
makes us leave the physical picture framing factory. Things we   saw
before we said so. Color is subjective, a baby verb in the adult.   *All
You Can Eat* pictured things when you're finished being hungry.   That's
America for you & for you. That's Japan in *Tomorrow's Thinking*   enter-
tainment, minted for exchange. I know because I'm always in the   wrong
time zone, in a honey sunset of life looking for a stranger's swimming   pool
to die in temporarily. Mother was beautiful & knew him. She too   painted.
When She Was Bad, I was bystander, *GAUZE, VASELINE*, gallery   visitor.
Honk if this makes you nervous or troubles that positive side of

aggression.

LOUISE BOURGEOIS' FATHER

relations can be anticipated and are eternal

If geometry falls at his feet, in over-looked time, his memory equation will
come to pass like bee's liquid color over the field of light, like the children
running from the rooms, their nanny dancing upside down inside his sleep,
or so like all, all his body parts dismembered & placed for a party on
the dining table, the once private bed, the table, the bed, that body born &
suffered, procreated & sexed, cheating in the years before memory, lied
about, lied from in the house, grabbed, now eaten & died, & swallowed &
soon suffered again inside the child's body. The child's skin is a field
giving up light every time it is hurt. See, the numbers just don't add up:
The mother is missing in the dark. The children have come to the dinner
table to be this quiet. After ten years of geometry between the rooms,
the nanny will leave the house, all ochre lights left on in the windows.
Art is better than geometry when it comes to deep function & duplicity of
a large father upside down in a home with a mother, children, with
a nanny. So, to destroy the father is to have the father, to undo. Then
becomes now, a subtraction of uncertain shapes & baby food colors, &
soon, the liquidated daughter wants to be the field devouring everlasting
light, named the one responsible for the father's final destruction, for
the fine laid table, for skin of the bed, twilight's fuck dust breathed
                                        before sleep.

LAVINIA FONTANA'S *CHILD OF THE MONKEY* IS SAID LOST

in a canopy-bearing past, her rainforest
falling unheard in my bedroom but for its laced
understory leafbed layering, death's close call. The painter-
mother's earthenware is baking & breaking, branch to branch
in the kitchen, as far down as the garden's deaf worm's only ear.
Say it.   You wish you were there, naked

naked in that room of her painting, in the real
timeframe it took her to really see you, monkey of the child,
hands like moth-lit candle wax holding up your Portuguese great-
grandmother's found letter saying she was lost, adopted from another
country. She wanted to be heard. Not home with Lavinia's 11 other children
speak-ing tongues or like a tamed wolf, fur-cheeked child in plaintive pain, commissioned.
Only women relatives were allowed to be portrayed naked, lavished first & last

outstanding by her brush, away from haloed-hot sun or forest-floor-warm mulch.
Say it.   I would not have come to you as a daughter handed over,
altarpiece, unclothed for a King. Rather, I'd come counterpart to
Aphrodite, in myrtle & rose-wash, hidden tail between my
legs like a tongue singing to say it in another language,
dark in pearl time. Said, Say it:
By the window, I mix my own paint,
but I don't want to be alone.

OF CAMILLE CLAUDEL'S BEGGAR CLOTHES

As if full-derived in waltz motion, as if wax-figured for hammer
heading for bronze, you'd think, conjured out of this nonexistence
feast, the body   becomes destination only, skin of another's folding
over for the heart's first & last harm. The anatomy   in parts displays
disassemble, believes its limbs have gone, genitals taken, organs all
vanished in feeling without permission, as if unarmed for uglier things
to come. To have constant cause to walk or dance, to unravel like cloth,
revolve in triple time across marble-dusted floors, around a glass table,
to disappear into thoughtless-cataclysm swoon & sinew-moves, a naked
curve: a consequence no one cares for, especially from a figure   that bears
plague & error of abandon, shape   missing its Gorgon's severed head, no
longer in tandem, hanging from the one red umbrella of her mind   opened.

Leaving the city's cleaved timeframe, we. Who

is allowed entrance. Our state's sheer-bagged oranges

spill out like planets at the endless groves'

desert's edge. *Now and then* the body measured time

in relation to others, not so giddy ago, giving back

what the mind got. Culture's quick robbery

                    of language & skin color took

The Long Memory's road, the rust cage out under

a downpour sky's output epiphany. You can still

hear breathing in the trees. Don't be fooled: Violence

still bleeds from a syrup bottle spilling over

the old globe. Sticky wicket. And

the stuffed bird's gunshot pellet falls like a quarter

in an unsightly slot machine, shows up

in your femur's X-Ray. Explain. Someone

will open under the chipped stars—her expression,

like a trout's blue gill-plate

after it's been caught & laid out there

       on fresh dirt.

...until the first feather touches the last one

and two black waves

meet in Vienna, outstretched, spread bride-like with Prussian
blue & a violated ecstasy of confusion. I look for Florence on
her map, applaud my daily daydream of him who has yet to come
to me. There will be a calendar of spells, incessant touching & cut
cry of a peacock imprisoned above the sea. No mechanical cure, no
collapsing piano act of liberation for me possible: *into the freedom
of her story* she comes, sees herself rise & rise from the bed's world-
tumult, tenderly. Two gold shoes have been left on a flight of stairs
in that garden. I knew they might begin to house wilderness dead
& live things, coming & going without me. So, for both of us, I
realize, in this cause & effect we ask from each other, there is no
limit to inquiry, ache, & precarious part. One mind is not like another:
kite, moth glove, straitjacket, hop-scotch squares, underwater door,

falling camera...

Scissors

"Everybody knows you always start with scissors"

AN OCTOPUS CAN SEE WITH ITS SKIN, MASAYO FUKUDA!

-Kirie (切り絵, literally 'cut picture')

I have to

 Kirie there where this skin swallows rain, where propeller-cut whales drown if down too long, my own head extinguished by smell of gasoline, its neon-lit station next to our house when I was four. But all time is like 50,000 spiders per acre in your year, those moon-blue fields rocking them, rocking them in the dry mouth of wind where a parliament of white owls watches, where ants never sleep.

Let me

 chew arsenic from apple & pear seed, become pale with goldfish kept in the dark too long, lose my balance from kindness, like a moth have no stomach, sleep behind one Japanese paper screen with toothpick boxes brim filled with Meliboeus beetles, lie on cardamom & coffee grounds with a dervish-numbered language of reason at the back of my throat like gemstones, cold from the cutting.

Just let me

 gillyflower from memory's chestnut on a fire, your fishing line tied around my ankles, scissors shining under black water. Not be bouquet mooring-light down in the box flowers' barbarity colors only, or in negative space surrounded by all-white, frail incandescent salt-outburst from swimming the ocean's rocking coffin, her sand haired doll's white wardrobe left eaten by flint silverfish, so lace-light shines through & freckles this floor under us until

         we cannot stand.

CAN CINDY SHERMAN | REALLY WEAR MY HAIR?

Not everyone | digs their own image. Some people | just feel
the shovel, this funerary smell of loose earth, art of the face.
My | gender is age, mirror in the mouth, an incurable look in the eyes,
French bridegroom | of admiration for you. Can you | blame |me?

For every white noise there's a washing machine & the dead weight
of your name| being pushed around town. There's a photograph to prove
it. I | am invention of burnt bread, the discontinued pose you asked of
me, whole night of singing. Can you circus act in color, grief-teach | yourself
how to dance out the floorboards away from the house into the fields again?

Make still this likeness from the last film's reverie. Instead of my own
misunderstood-blue figurine | falling from a great height as I held unlaced
breath, appeared for fakery, used & unscathed cameo. | Un-Sexed for sweet
strange. Uncertain birth motif doing often as & little as they | can. Guise | is
a living in thus-far supine beauty | if you could ask for a substitute. | Come
closer. You, not you: | To my spirited self-portrait | be true.

JENNY SAVILLE?

Can't compare this company of painted strangers to only ancestors,
abstract & figurative together, one too-many legs overhanging, too
many arms slung from a child's body carried out of the next War brew.
   Collapsing in close contact, coupling in flux, confront her stare
   one tempera part at a time: ear to vagina, delft blue carotid artery
   pulled from the neck as the lover's brain is about to say what it
   shouldn't. It's Pieta-time again. Three Fates will intertwine now
   as if then, holding her form flat down onto a mirror, to *hold*
   the image down until it gives in, until it gives up its otherwise-life
   back, disrupting. Women & women give birth, God the moment,
   a narrative in endless flesh propped high on the chair with big knees
   from above. When slipping her pink tongue into the mouth of another
they dissolve passage like sliding down the polished home banister backwards
to an unlit hall landing. But who we are as adults is lost on us who sees them-
selves only ugly, lost on that original child who, sexless, once saw herself whole.

A MARTINE GUTIERREZ TRIAD
—for my Dylan Tara

Angel, | are you
drowning your bedsheets' song skins in
the moon's pool water for a better *muse-muse*, for a *body in thrall?*
We wake against feeling like worn party undergarments torn out &
garden-buried, cut fruit thrown at the foot | of the front wood door, their
fire candied colors crushed from an insect's head. . .

　　　To be deity-desire, | polished chrome, or coughed-up sun
aureate occupied by breath is everything. As if otherwise was a beauty
choice every tribe recognizes. I'm my son, the girl | he wants to be—so,
kiss these genders in us, find each naked mannequin twin | in the crowd,
a fish-mask breathing under our dining table downing all the last light.
We're just one flame | thrown, tied hair to leaves into feathers & for
a pierced, jeweled-hungry face, | knowing perfection will always

be sexless. I'd cross
over, again & again any day to make her feel safe, crawl inside carved
base of a tree, | meet wet anemone's brooding for its pink & green axle |
revolving in the sea's seat place, let him be her, them, in the visa-versa,
be uncured of expectation for wild dancing. *Hands up*—
We're original owner of this one body | & I want you to see it.

I stood up, willed for | nothing. I looked into this watercourse until she looked
back & remembered me holding out the scissors, their albatross wings, this | face
off frame. It becomes first-hand easy parse of pain, its hands in there, in
the far & near rib & waist girth measurements I'm familiar with | soul's sink
hole that houses these rake feelings. It's familiar. It's old family. What you have
once done, common as a warehouse full of flat hand-sized moths clouding the high
windows, keeping the coughed-up quiet. Measurement there. An | appetite for it, for
death & wet sex in us, the clear & present danger-collaboration between two or more
people. I punchbowl-float on the sea, sleep & pray no | error there remains, keeps them,
the family all together in the same room just long enough to | kill a burden you can still
believe in. You can female-   smudge long enough for a *Genetic longing* that pulls hard
at my ponytail & keeps me out of dusk's spilled gold, from flies in the hayloft corral nightly.
I am as unprecedented, precise, a staircase creak: know this, keep what you know close,
quarreling in the mind: there's an act, a stone in a drawer, this thought said   ordinary.

WITHOUT HOKUSAI'S GREAT WAVE 1760-1849
THERE WOULD BE NO MODERN ART

—*Angus Lockyer*

& no Rothko's sand blue over brown, incalculable equation to grind
paint between
your teeth. I hear night's shore pouring its black gravel over
my head,
embedded mica flecks shining under the one eye that refuses to close.
Laughter is
exile's closet partner, anger's better half, gutted. No gray backwashed
sister ribbed
& undressed in the moraine ravine filled with flood, or a fallen cow's
bloated belly-
suffering another morning's wet heat. Paper boats set sail when
you commerce:
Sea spray unlike blown snow in her drift. No accidental love or
revolution. *No Rat*
and salmon goodnight story, piece of rope for hanging on. Without his
Great Wave,
Masculine Wave, Feminine Wave. There would be no confusion as
what had
to come next. The sea is never late coming home as it is.
Without him,
no photo soup kitchen, no lover's mother impression left in her
only tossed
coffin box the size of one shoe floating between kelp blades, pod
bladders, soda
ash wash & November's green pin cushion of rain. There would be no
woodblock sound,
no murdered Kohada Koheiji bone & flack skin ghost pulling back his
mosquito net `

for us to see Hokusai's wife & new lover—putting to bed the night's
vanishing boat's
heavy cargo overboard. I know what the shore bottom's shadow is
like, not to breathe
or breathe twice there, because the greater sea only wants to live.

UNDERWATER BILL VIOLA & UNDERWATER WITH YOU

It depends on where the coined air comes between you, me,

your cry, where tipped-white water falls to fall from each limb,
a crowned afternoon letting go of its memory, you.
Your child body slipped quiet beside death into a stilled lake
beneath its mountain surrounding, saw his new buried world rut,
beautiful there. All rain becomes sea, births a lake, becomes river,
now water, as if this water was liquid window opening out, out into
light that already broke from the gape-face of a blue orchid in another
country, moaned around the ankles of the one standing bedside beside
you in the willing dark as if to help your sleep-breathing live a little longer.
Invisible heavens will keep time climbing up inside your leg bones, water's
baritone-move swooning the room. A father will never be brother, brother
never lover, lover not the mother a ship you climb back into to find cyan
brushstroke's horizon just past that sea's farthest tripwire end line where

the self-annihilating, far, all deflowering sun then somehow escapes daily.

Mother is still drowning in an acre-green ocean made from

wet firing squad blindfolds. She's the gone money I can't stop

giving away. She is gone, except in the returning rhetoric

of sleep. No one will ask you to turn your back to a mirror to see

yourself in yourself. The heart is one dome-immortal jellyfish

pulsing the hurting ribcage hours. No one will ask you. It's

money under the sand pillow when you sleep: you wake with

pulled baby teeth. No one will ask you to give her to memory

because she's already there, eaten by sea clouds on the event horizon.

If you can paint anything, you could be someone else, you can repeat

yourself, find your way back. Know, jellyfish have no brains,

Mother, no more feelings now than the ones I red-tide remember

receiving—I hang them, I keep them as counterfeit notes

for the one ink-dark day when all bets are off.

ALBRECHT DÜRER'S MOTHER WAS HALF-DRAWN
AS A GIRAFFE, 1514:

a gourd head that protruded hard death toward the bone door, that long
    afterwards-animal growing face & limb out of her there. I hated all
    limits of being human, climbing avocado trees, flying & kicking free
    from the sea's pitch & fetch, then covering my body entire in hot
    grey sand like a second rough skin. The German word "Haut"
means skin, hide, a defense, shelter, the kind you can carry around or peel from
bed of another body to wear or used as window coverings not intended
to either see in or out from. Other rooms, not meant to hear, understood
my parents, how their sheets smelled best when hung out for
the garden's late wind. A backyard can equally house perfect feel
    of pillow & Indian rhino, nocturnal red-brown stag beetle clinging to
    the moon's only swinging bed sheet like a child's imperfect logic. Child
    of me wanted & wanted Dürer's torn parrot's wing for hand, uncaged
brown *Osterhase* hare at rest on the white page of a mother's forgiveness.

MOTHERWELL BLACK

—a teaspoon of blackhole weighs the same as a planet

                            I'm inside
the painter's room   that keeps getting bigger. Standing
one Rorschach test away from ochre. Another, not much farther
from shoelace green. I'm standing three flag sheets to the wind,
three black holes   really, holding hands like concealed
revolvers
at the hip, holding hands at this open door's   windless dark matter.
A foreskin-pink elephant in the room is too large to see me there.
Because this room   keeps getting bigger, repeating itself in untitled
years, in a "conspiracy of silence." Because maternal love is meant
to be echo-endless, something you want to throw yourself down into.
Because I'd throw myself in front of a revolver for them, dropping coins
like pulled fingernails or the memory of stars, still holding hands in
Spanish Franco's frozen streets   just to see black.

DISTANCE IS ALTERED BY TIME, JOAN JONAS,

like a B film now animated by *bat-like thought-wings...*

Take measure from the ground up. Fall over your female shadow

there, come fairytale for it. As if that wasn't time's own vertigo

ghosting under a stone's all glacier green. *Organic Honey's Visual Telepathy*

where a vertical roll timeframe draws the line between then and now.

The long pause we make of ourselves looking, like a circle's *delay, delay,* slow

turning as Andrena bees from breathing. Across a sunflower's sum, Fibonacci

numbers where you can predict sequence, childhood has a child able to have

children. There's no minor theater birds stilling themselves in the storm of

these hours. Wind, dandelion listener. We measure ourselves by what we see.

Running up over the risers, look ahead, through the transparent architecture of

the past, a girl-boy in *Reanimation* again, toward the mirror's one crawl space

to stop time or finally put an end to how they'll look at you.

BARBARA KRUGER & THE GOLDILOCKS ZONE

The difference between "enough" and "all"

—BIN RAMKE

With *half pity & half patience* I made the decision at ten I was born
missing, Native American, not of my parents.   Cleaved. Could I cross
a bear's darkness-river on horseback? Twice occur out of vision with
counter-knowledge, escape the differences between, back out
of the cliché of being female. I could be a   male bedded there in that

word, declare himself first to the moon's poudrin table, take a larger chair.
His   *Demi-acquaintance* made me cry under the bed, confide in my closet
though I was never afraid of death or stitches sewn on the open shirt.
Visible is what others are, not what   I wanted to be: ally only
to myself, obliterated-free enough, never sleeping for   any badlands.
Daughter of light & its late consequences, the past had a way of speaking
to me in coy candor. Common sense was not as strong as the other senses,
not stupid enough to make me believe in a future.   It all belonged to
someone else like my parents who could see it, unsightly as drawn
boundaries & the swig-violence of adults.

HIERONYMUS BOSCH'S
VERTIGO BUTT MUSIC DRAWN

But all dark notes are dismantled there from the middle ear, downward.
Voyaged mind, cauldron skin I knew. Can you claim anything is yours?

The burning salt hour throws its black broken glass frame skyward. Left
behind the mum orchestra, my parts in peril & my animals dizzy for

lust past all lost astronomy & wipe-out, this naked edible overjoy, a suicide
in syllables, fifth panic, fourth stall's birds-fermata, this half ocean's

susurrus still coming over me in the picture. Can you akin? Can you hear it,
pinned to the unseasonable underearth, an option for music & water constantly

changing shape, an answer in dissonance? To hear desire is to wake yourself
inside, upturned long enough to know tomorrow is exile. Chaos, body harp &

painted butt music, crowd-crawl, rose crowned to the chest, rabbit call &
playing cards . . . Listen, I'm hell-humming in your direction, giddy, am too-

taken to leave it alone, this will be locked in as if it is already inside of me
now: to fall. Let's be clear my darling azure from the reeling crave, your

spilled gut-platter of enclosed bones in its final flesh-clean drop, it so
sounds inhale-like all my lovers on fire, rising with the cliff's updraft!

ALMOST HARUNOBU

Black wings
of hair, Binsashi bone pins, women of me come now servant to
the Tama river, washing courtesan brocade, multi-coloured on
a screen, new lovers kneeling. She too turns cinnabar-red by hand
paint, vertical to horizontal, lost memory sheets showing months.

That court gives rank for autumn & winter after a milk
bath in front of the mosquito's net, musical motif, when this
advent-end of the 17th century pulls back the bow. When

you first costume, when home, play *Janken* & story straw, kyudo
already exists for the target ahead. What pattern of singing still
rises from this color page & reaches you in secret? How I see yields
no temperament, eyes half-closed, not looking up when walking off
this shunga landscape. Butterfly halo above trees, kimono sleeves open,
hands each to each holding & beneath my obi fold, a hidden dinner

bell underwater, the clit sex-knot, this impermanence of
hello or farewell like violence rhythmed in the mind
$$\text{after war.}$$

DISAPPEARANCE IS FRANCESCA WOODMAN'S PROVIDENCE

Map   of movements, my shadow takes its timeframes from me,

becomes how far to go from the wallpaper's arsenic flower for

the fetish of what is missing. After all, the wall can be coffin-like

when my body is left alone against time, merging with the oblique

imagination, with my hurting organs that have no music heard.

To seek containment's corners, closed windows, cupboard, hinged

door, counter, curtains…the way we make a thing of ourselves

happen, auto-erotic, auto-prophetic. But one hand will not hold water,

nor the eye, another's locked gaze for long. *With the end of my breath—*

is the beginning of yours like a tin tea kettle left to boil down in

another room. Away we came to this antumbra-place with private

thinking shifting paper, light above, copper Japanese beetles

hatching under the earth below. But the wind, like nothing, rocks

inside us the same as truth. A lover cannot escape this   vertigo.

ITS ORIGIN FLOWING THROUGH THE LIMBS,
LEONARDO DA VINCI

or insensibly, *in the middle of the surface of the earth* in one muscle direction
he came vicinity. He, like Master-God thinking, studied-out autumn light's late

groundwater course down to my feet, already his. Light was all the skin's hit,
circle & double of me there, proof apparent. My face, that flanked Italian

centuries past a kiss, remained lawless form. He drew my limb length on
every church wall, came candlelight-side & locked a stare back, made memory's

pupils dilate their crypt. I knew I was what I felt, *more obtuse in the new* as this painted
flesh persisted to shine outside-strange, wet instrument organ of slow

breathing with red sea horses, drunken-teetering in their shade behind my curled
hippocampus-cage's own shadow. He, covet & anguish, he, pirate of my wreck,

covered one eye to see me better. He, of *the cause of lust and other appetites of
the body* could not be found of sound mind. Hear me? I was already his olio-

anatomy measure. Hear? Sight's many undertakings made red sketch for
perfection. My made carapace held the strange color of empty church pews

filled with stained glass fallen. Fucking hell. Look: No one came to pray. No
one came, otherwise-worship to sing!

IN FOR RAUSCHENBERG'S DANTE
—voting

Please.
       Based on this cut-out transfer, crude, my one

sorrow head might have it, face down, soaked in lighter

fluid, let this vex day count for our threshold to home,

an itinerary epitome-me you saw in yourself shake the history

shroud over our fire balcony. Can you see that fine Circle of Hell

punishment smile from the Mona & the Lisa, from the void oasis?

Is it really a bullying look-in-the-eye you still want? Rubbed by

the low coal of exit-dawn's everyday smudge in newspaper-grey,

one false kiss emerges, killing thousands. A foregone conclusion.

A familiar object into paint. The sky overhead is made of blue jay

feathers & mocking. Free water below soon becomes a wagon road

of dry canto stones I cannot count. My unknown neighbor walks

knee-deep in its absence there where a white, white, white fence

is implied by silence as I beg my dead dad to lift me up over.

& they die & they price on request, runaway, they frequent
as the fashion brain can Kanye, as conceptual keeps its eye on
Africa hurt, face-down. How fast can you stare at each other in
a full room of people? | Let's say she can swallow caviar as easy as
a water-mourned river stone the color of skin. | Let's say I bury it in
a sentence you recognize full of other sentences giving birth out of
strapped air & need to be heard when the news has just dropped
the next dummy bomb (dummy picture included). | Let's say there's so
many of us are naked or in bathing suits the color of decomposing time,
locked in stance. Suffering (an auction) paints the all-inside
of the skull the way a two-year-old draws on a wall. You are hard to get
when it comes to remembering what must come next. Oh yeah: it's always
your luck body first & last, lasting until it doesn't. | Bella, its small army
inside of you won't stand down, sleepless as format speech, won't listen.

PANIC AT JOHN BALDESSARI'S KISS

The aftermath, always happening, an airplane falling, a man
mid-air falling from a horse, & an arrow, a gun pointing away,
at us, our all bulls-eye-on-the-mark. This is what he sees
when he sees. Maybe *Wrong* or not, the appropriation, the film
clip, chase, pressed lips over lips, photo moment on the minute-drawn
breath in, the over, the under, bodies in black & white cut to pose,
the way a kiss can pose, dispose of everything around it for another,
dispose of thinking. It's like waving good-bye. Mouth to mouth seeing
as saying. Inside. Resuscitation back to the brain saying *yes* as the mouth
makes an O. Circles for the digital age, colored dots for faces already
made for erasing. Hurry, come, he, 6'7", sees fifteen minutes from the
Mexican border cremates his old paintings up-close. But the ashes were
kept in a book urn, not so afloat in the ocean with my parents, *Above, On
and Under (with Mermaid)* to kiss & kiss, riot in the dark depth of it.
The collision, the kiss, the capture, once in the for-all-we-know of
haunting who comes first. Kiss into kiss & so into kiss. All laws
of gravity leave us. Gender begins in violence & space. Space begins
in gender & violence as all laws of gravity leave us. So, kiss, kiss, kiss!

POETRY'S SUBSTANCE ABUSE
IS A DARWIN FINCH DRAWING

in motion, or error of abandon

                              when you least expect it, much like when

they say your next love will come to you when you least expect it, your

face stopping there at the equatorial bulge because its pull at either

seam is one continuous seamount ring of fire already put out on your

head, leaving you somewhere vocabulary-continuum-caught on pause,

the pause button same as the mute button, same as all faith in God is no god,

same as you are your last thought swallowed silver before it's said out-loud to

a tiny hand mirror sleeping in the involuntary dark inside your purse, big

enough for the birdcage thrown out in that alley trash heap, its past songs

now more a consequence of gravity than feathers' defiance. Perfect is your

animal shape's imperfection-in-the-making, every dark matter's silent

distribution shape & origin-tangle: Sweet physical chaos, make

                              whatever creates unequal harm.

TIEPOLO'S ALLEGORY OF THE PLANETS & CONTINENTS CEILING

I'll arrive at the faces in motion, unfinished.
Cloud in cello billow, pale-fallen from the frame,
heavens closing in. Action is his paint recognition.
Four continents from which to turn your head. From which to turn away.
   To beast Time back from rapture. We are not new
to this scene, our era of undoing. This feeling I get down here:
when grackles suddenly leave their tree, congregate air's final
teal act of trickery: breaking back of ocean, dusk-blur between its grief-pink &
   twilight skin of relic blue, what pulled submission
to yellow & grey as this god raised his one arm & bares
his chest against our chests breathing too hard, replicated
once before our forefathers died. But no one I know,
   everyone is fixed in this orbit of doing, going
waltz, corium's incoherent wheel-labor & pleasure's turning:
connected & accounted for. Time in cello's billow.

KAZUKI TAKIZAWA'S COLOR FROM GREEN

Brain, love-shelled
beginning in this fine desire engine-metronome breath
between breath, stay intact. Tell me my color today & those
I left light-behind in childhood on shore—they were made of

mother's collected glass, now tiny inedible grains of sand, now live
shells carrying other bodies out to sea to a Pacific shelf downed by no
sun. Out of silence you make language my own, a transparency I can
hold up until this air becomes too heavy or rain fills my voice with its
own gray need to sing. Reclaim me. Fold me home. Carry me out of your

kiln, cooling, this blown shape, dawn shimmering in my sides. Because talk
begins in heat in the form as one passenger who never leaves the moving
train, as the *senbazuru* cranes' wings fold back to you in silence, circling
the hour, I can only hear them and the exhale-wind between the long
bird-ribs in these trees.

NOTES

Italicized lines in poems, not otherwise identified, belong to the artist

Pg.8 Andy Goldsworthy's Sticks & Stones

His work involves using natures materials to build outdoor sculptures that usually fall apart and become weather worn as in nature. I love that he was also former professor of applied mathematics; "Each work grows, stays, decays—"

Pg.9 A Walkabout in Andrew Wyeth's Painting

Many of the paintings' surrounding expansive landscapes, fields, and skies, first caught my focal attention . . . as did his title "Squall." I spent much of my life near the ocean and it was the implied emotion, overall color-feeling of longing and depression that was carried there, sometimes like a guilt-ridden memory. The woman I gave directions to, likely a neighbor's housekeeper, was taken away in an ambulance. I never found out if she survived the accident. *Walkabout* refers to one of my favorite early films by Nicolas Roeg, 1971.

Pg.10 *What War is This*, Laurie Anderson?

inspired by her 2019 Grammy-winning album & video: https://www.youtube.com/watch?v=MlVXBxAuDGw Laurie Anderson & Kronos Quartet—The Water Rises / Our Street is a Black River referring to hurricane Sandy.

Pg.11 Turner, Strapped to the Mast

A bireme is an ancient oared warship (galley) with two decks of oars, invented and used by Greeks, even before the 6th century B.C. "Biremes were long vessels built for military purposes, had relatively high speed.

Pg.13 Rachel Whiteread: It's So

This is about my half-sister Lynne's death by drowning and how it ties to our recent immigration crisis with so many lost at sea trying to reach safe harbors in other countries. Whiteread's past work with boxes and casting of large negative spaces seem a perfect metaphor for the grief aligned with my experience of isolation.

Pg.16 Hannah Hoch: Everything Me Was Unmoored Object
Hannah was one of the earliest female Dada artists. She was also one of my earliest influences.
Dada originally meant "hobby-horse"; *Die Puppen*, or *The Dolls*, is the title of one of Hoch's works for her handmade puppets.

Pg.23 Dalí's Recipe Dead: Politics
A true story of my daughter seeing a sun-bathing girl on a huge lawn in Stuyvesant town; the young woman did not notice the falcon tearing apart its pigeon! All italicized lines belong to Salvadore Dalí from his marvelous, bizarre, sometimes horrifying, illustrated 1973 cookbook *Les diners de Gala*. The epigraph line seemed especially apt for our present political situation. Salpicon is a dish of one or more ingredients diced or minced and bound with a sauce or liquid.

Pg.24 Fritz Kahn's Machine Body Survives 2018 in a Sarcophagus
Artist/ doctor who made wild conjecture-illustrations. His phantom imaginings and mechanical designs of human body organs provided unlikely juxtapositions and somehow led me to one of our recent political horror-stories: Kavanaugh being made Supreme Court Judge.

Pg.27 At Age 6, Marina Abromović Began Living with her Parents
She has been on the scene and on my radar a long time. Saw her when I was a child: unnerving.
Kerf—a slit made by cutting with a saw.

Pg.28 Francis Bacon Swallows the Head Whole
for my half-sister Lynne who died after her car washed off the Topanga Canyon cliffs in a rainstorm; she was found a week later with remade (remaking appearance) appearance—Bacon's phrase to describe his portraits.

Gabion—cage full of rocks often used in geological projects to prevent landslides. Hebenon—the botanical poison thought to be used in *Hamlet*

Pg.29 Pierre Huyghe's Crab Wore My Sleeping Mask
—from *Zoodram 5 (after 'Sleeping Muse' by Constantin Brancusi)*, (2011)
Brian Kim Stephans/ *Humanities* 2017, 6 (1), 9; doi: 10.3390/h6010009
Article The New Commodity: Technicity and Poetic Form: Marx's cursory linking of Darwin's evolutionary theories and the history of the "productive organs of society" anticipates the central, distinctive theme of Simondon's philosophy: that technology develops through history toward greater states of *concretization*, perhaps a form of "perfection," that resembles the progress of life forms through time toward a greater fitness with a given environment—a *milieu*, or, in the language of Uexküll, *Umwelt*.
—from ART NEWS: October 2013 pg.98 "The retrospective itself is perhaps best conceived of as, to use UexKull's word once again, an *umwelt*, a 'sense island,' significant environnment," or 'cognitive map." –Christopher Mooney

Pg.34 Why *All Portraits Are A Form of Taxidermy*, Ricardo Nicolayevsky
Italicized portion of the title is a statement derived from a *BOMB* magazine article 128/ Summer 2014 Artists on Artists, by Luis Felipe Fabre, translated from the Spanish by Camino Detorrela; The English Walter Potter (1835-1918) was probably the most famous taxidermist. He had a museum that included some fantastical scenes and bizarre creatures including two-headed lambs and four-legged chickens.

Pg.35 Where is Dead Artist Jack Goldstein?
Jack was a long-time family friend and my mother's lover; his art became part of my thinking-upbringing.

Pg.36 Caitlin Berrigan's Transfer Cultural Despair-Wear
from: http://caitlinberrigan.com
A cosmology that draws upon geology to investigate how deep time and interspecies communication might assist us in radical planetary transformation. Comprised of video, sculpture and communication

instruments, *Imaginary Explosions* explores what other presents and futures become possible once we begin to think beyond the framework of the human. The pseudo-science fictions work across episodic videos, sculptures, costumes and drawings that forge into affective geologies and the idea of becoming mineral...given the eco-threats we are facing.

Pg.39 The Hat We Cannot Put on is Full of Honey: Ann Hamilton
Ann Hamilton, one of my personal iconic artists and generous inspiration as she gave me two images for my last two books.
Clade: a group of organisms believed to have evolved from a common ancestor.

Pg.40 No Suspending Bruce Nauman
used chairs, suspended chairs, and made references to chairs in many of his works. Nauman's "ambiguous" (Tate gallery website) word-image lithograph was part of his palindrome, anagram, mirror-image pieces of the 70's. David Pagel's essay, *Bruce Nauman*, describes the artist's "language's real force derives from the claim it makes on embodied speakers . . . this perverse request . . . implicates his body." Yet he later admits that the title's
"abbreviation for the anagram when its last three letters are read as the abbreviation for the French word madame. Although this shift in reference prevents the speaker from requesting his own [violence] victimization, it does so only by transferring this fate to an anonymous woman." . . . fate??
Bruce Nauman Edited by Robert C Morgan, pg.203, PAJ Books, 2002 John Hopkins University Press.

Doppel-gänger double walker as in woman raped becomes an "other," distanced into a double, forced to walk and back out into the world—for the *Me Too* anonymous-us-them, anonymous and not anonymous, because we all belong to this/ a collective language, not just as an art object, "currency of the imagination" (Jeanette Winterson) exchanged in the art bargain. For me, a clear consequence-breakdown of language.

Pg.49 Jessica Grindstaff Brought Back my Phantom Limb
Grindstaff's art company is called "Phantom Limb"; gratitude is due for

the notional concept, even the book's giving over to ekphrasis, combined with childhood memories, and/or political fevers that made for perfect unforeseen appendages. Memory is an ever-changing appendage.

In theoretical physics, phantom fields are obtained usually as solutions to field equations. . . . An alternative source of repulsive gravity in the context of exotic fields would be represented by a distribution with negative energy density, i.e., a phantom field. In fact, comparison with observational data... suggests that a phantom field can explain the acceleration of our Universe. – *Geometrothermodynamics of phantom AdS black holes.*
Hernando Quevedo, María N. Quevedo, Alberto Sánchez

Pg.50 Ed Ruscha First Blew the Dirty Whistle
Hollywood is a Verb is Ruscha's title––tense changed; my parents knew him at Chouinard Art Institute where Father taught drawing for most of his long career.

Pg.53 Of Camille Claudel's Beggar's Clothes
The title emerged from recorded stories on how the artist appeared after being cast aside by Rodin and rejected by her family, therefore, being forced into poverty; she was seen wearing *beggar's clothes*. Many references are made to her astonishing sculptures.

Pg.55 Coming Between Rebecca Horn & Her Film
I could have written 10 poems on her work, as she is definitely one of my favorite artists in this series. "To talk about love is like a wind that I shield off with a fan. It stubbornly seeks its own course and quite uncontrollably attacks me." Rebecca Horn

Pg.61 A Martine Gutierrez Triad
Sea anemones, because they breed asexually...for my beautiful Dylan whose liminal form is love.

Pg.68 Distance is Altered by Time, Joan Jonas
My bat-like thought-wings would beat painfully in that sudden searchlight - H.D.
The titles and references are taken from this Joan Jonas 2016 interview:

Layers of Time
https://www.youtube.com/watch?v=WISIYE4dOKw&ab_channel=
LouisianaChannel

Pg.69 Barbara Kruger & The Goldilocks Zone
half pity & half patience belongs to poet Brendan Constantine; *Demi-acquaintance* belongs to Barbara Kruger; *Visible is what others are* belongs to poet Bin Ramke

Pg.74 In for Rauschenberg's Dante
knee-deep in its absence: a quote from Wendell Berry's *The Never Ending Fire*

Pg.79 Kazuki Takizawa's Color from Green
Heavenly human and brilliant artist with whom I hope to take more classes.

SECTIONS: ROCK / PAPER / SCISSORS /
In 2006, American federal judge Gregory Presnell from the Middle District of Florida ordered opposing sides in a lengthy court case to settle a trivial (but lengthily debated) point over the appropriate place for a deposition using the game of rock–paper–scissors.[36][37] The ruling in *Avista Management v. Wausau Underwriters* stated: Upon consideration of the Motion—the latest in a series of Gordian knots that the parties have been unable to untangle without enlisting the assistance of the federal courts—it is ORDERED that said Motion is DENIED.

NY TIMES Article By CAROL VOGEL APRIL 29, 2005 https://www.nytimes.com/2005/04/29/arts/design/rock-paper-payoff-childs-play-wins-auction-house-an-art-sale.html It may have been the most expensive game of rock, paper, scissors ever played. Takashi Hashiyama, president of Maspro Denkoh Corporation, an electronics company based outside of Nagoya, Japan, could not decide whether Christie's or Sotheby's should sell the company's art collection, which is worth more than $20 million, at next week's auctions in New York.

He did not split the collection—which includes an important Cézanne landscape, an early Picasso street scene and a rare van Gogh view from the artist's Paris apartment—between the two houses, as sometimes happens. Nor did he decide to abandon the auction process and sell the paintings through a private dealer.

Mr. Maclean's 11-year-old twins, Flora and Alice, turned out to be the experts Ms. Ishibashi was looking for. They play the game at school, Alice said, "practically every day."

"Everybody knows you always start with scissors," she added.
"Rock is way too obvious, and scissors beats paper." Flora piped in.
"Since they were beginners, scissors was definitely the safest," she said, adding that if the other side were also to choose scissors and another round was required, the correct play would be to stick to scissors—
because, as Alice explained, "Everybody expects you to choose rock."

The first known mention of the game was in the book *Wuzazu* [zh] by the Chinese Ming-dynasty writer Xie Zhaozhi [zh] (fl. c. 1600), who wrote that the game dated back to the time of the Chinese Han dynasty (206 BC – 220 AD).[7]

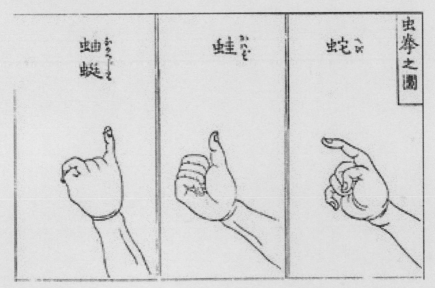

Mushi-ken, the earliest Japanese sansukumi-kengame (1809). From left to right: slug (namekuji), frog (kawazu) and snake (hebi).

Throughout Japanese history there are frequent references to *sansukumi-ken*, meaning *ken* (fist) games where "the three who are afraid of one another" (i.e. A beats B, B beats C, and C beats A).[8] This type of game originated in China before being imported to Japan and subsequently also becoming popular among the Japanese.

ACKNOWLEDGMENTS

Many thanks to the journals in which these poems first appeared, sometimes in different versions.

A Constellation of Kisses: A Terrapin Books Anthology: "Panic at John Baldessari's Kiss"

Another Chicago Magazine: "Metronome Maple & Betye Saar," "Firing Squad, Convergence, Jackson Pollock"

Beloit Poetry Journal: "My Farewell Face & One of Picasso's"

Blackbird: "Tony Oursler & His Watchers Live On," "Francis Bacon Swallows the Head Whole"

Black Renaissance Noire: "An Octopus Can See with its Skin, Masayo Fukuda!"

BOMB: "The Hat We Cannot Put on is Full of Honey: Ann Hamilton"

The Chattahoochee Review: "Underwater Bill Viola & Underwater with You," "Howardena

Pindell to be Seen What Remains," "Bernini's Barbarous Gold Wing When Father," "Of Camille Claudel's Beggar Clothes"

Circus Noir: Poetry Circus # 6 (Chapbook) Yak Press, July 13, 2019, Ed. Nicelle Davis

Reprint of "Disappearance is Francesca Woodman's Providence," credit: *Denver Quarterly*

Denver Quarterly: "Rachel Whiteread: It's So," "Joseph Beuys Once Liked America the Coyote," "Disappearance is Francesca Woodman's Providence," "Coming Between Rebecca Horn & Her Film"

Entropy: "Caitlin Berrigan's Transfer Cultural Despair-Wear"

Full Blede: "Cloning Duchamp is Mathematics"

Image Journal: "Andy Goldsworthy's Sticks & Stones"

Interlitq: "A Martine Gutierrez Triad" & "Lynda Benglis, We're Cooked in LA"

Kyoto Journal: "Kazuki Takizawa's Color from Green"

Lana Turner: "Tiepolo's Allegory of the Planets & Continents Ceiling," "Louise Bourgeoise's Father"

Los Angeles Review: "Lavinia Fontana's *Child of the Monkey* is Said Lost"

Narrative Magazine: "If contents in /Joseph Cornell's Box," "Hannah Hoch: Everything Me Was Unmoored Object," and "A Walkabout in Andrew Wyeth's Painting"

New American Writing: "Pierre Huyghe's Crab Wore My Sleeping Mask," "Albrecht Dürer's Mother was Half-Drawn as a Giraffe, 1514"

Plume: "Awol Erizku's Rescued High Cactus," "Without Hokusai's Great Wave, There Would be No Modern Art," "Turner Strapped to the Mast, 1969," "Jessica Grindstaff Brought Back This Phantom Limb, "Its Origin Flowing Through the Limbs, Leonardo da Vinci," "Ed Ruscha First Blew the Dirty Whistle."

Plume 2022 (Featured Poet): "Poetry's Substance Abuse is a Darwin Finch Drawing," "Why *All Portraits Are a Form of Taxidermy*, Ricardo Nico-layevsky," "Style of Imprisonment: Diane Arbus Predicted This Virus," "Jenny Saville?" "Andrei Tarkovsky: Reckoning the Water Raft," and "Which War is This, Laurie Anderson?"

Plume Anthology 9: "Magritte's Forged Bank Notes"

Plume Anthology 10: "Dalí's Glutton Recipe Dead: Politics"

Poetry: "Panic at Baldessari's Kiss," "Hieronymus Bosch's Vertigo Butt Music Drawn"

Scoundrel Time: "Mike Kelley, Kelley Cheat Sheet," "It's Time Damien Hirst Died in the Pillbox"

Tribes.org: "Nan Goldin Fucks with 2020 Mirrors," "Instead, the Head Lor-na Simpson"

Verse Daily: reprint of "Underwater Bill Viola & Underwater with You" from *The Chattahoochee Review*

Volt: "Fritz Kahn's Machine Body Survives 2018 in a Sarcophagus," "In for Rauschenberg's Dante," "Before the Cock Crows Memento Mori: Cara-vaggio," "Can Cindy Sherman Really Wear My Hair?"

Vox Populi: "A Repeating Dream I'm Belly-Down at Eleven, Gerhard Rich-ter," "Artist Sophie Calle, Now Take Care of Yourself," "Marlene Dumas: World Evil is Banal," "At Age 6, Marina Abromović Began Living with

Her Parents," "Distance is Altered by Time, Joan Jonas," and "K: Vanessa Beecroft's Bodies Multiply"
Western Humanities Review: "Andrei Tarkovsky: Reckoning the Water Raft" "Why All Portraits Are a Form of Taxidermy, Ricardo Nicholayevsky"

For my stunning children Dylan, Chloe, & stepdaughter Merlin, and son-in-law Andrew, all, whose love and wisdom re-invents what it means to be in this world; my brother Stephen who defines art . . . and to my dearest friends who ignite my life daily. Special thanks to my astonishing editor, poet Rusty Morrison and Omnidawn Publishing's hard-working, inspired crew.

Gratitude to the brilliant artist William Wegman for the Cover Art Photo: William Wegman *Untied On, Tied Off,* 1973

ABOUT THE AUTHOR

 Former Regional Director of the Poetry Society of America, Elena Karina Byrne is a freelance editor and lecturer, Poetry Consultant & Moderator for *The Los Angeles Times* Festival of Books, poetry programs curator for the Craft Contemporary Museum, and Literary Programs Director for the historic Ruskin Art Club. A Pushcart Prize recipient, Elena's other publications include *If No Don't* (What Books Press, 2020), *Squander* (Omnidawn, 2016), *MASQUE* (Tupelo Press, 2008), and *The Flammable Bird,* (Zoo Press, 2002). Her poems have appeared in *Poetry, Best American Poetry, The Paris Review, Kyoto Journal, Verse Daily, Plume, BOMB,* and elsewhere. She's working on screenplays, short stories, and a collection of hybrid essays entitled *Voyeur Hour: Poetry, Art, Film, & Desire.*

If This Makes You Nervous
Elena Karina Byrne

Cover art by William Wegman, *Untied On Tied Off*, 1973, Silver Gelatin Print
Image courtesy of Marc Selwyn Fine Art

Cover and interior typeface: Adobe Jenson Pro.

Cover and interior design by adam b. bohannon

Printed in the United States
by Books International, Dulles, Virginia
On Glatfelter 50# Cream Natures Book 440 ppi
Acid Free Archival Quality Recycled Paper

Publication of this book was made possible in part by gifts from
Katherine & John Gravendyk in honor of Hillary Gravendyk,
Francesca Bell, Mary Mackey, and The New Place Fund

Omnidawn Publishing
Oakland, California
Staff and Volunteers, Fall 2021

Rusty Morrison & Ken Keegan, senior editors & co-publishers
Kayla Ellenbecker, production editor & poetry editor
Rob Hendricks, editor for *Omniverse*, marketing, fiction & post-pub publicity
Sharon Zetter, poetry editor & book designer
Liza Flum, poetry editor
Matthew Bowie, poetry editor
Anthony Cody, poetry editor
Jason Bayani, poetry editor
Gail Aronson, fiction editor
Laura Joakimson, marketing assistant for Instagram & Facebook, fiction editor
Ariana Nevarez, marketing assistant & *Omniveres* writer, fiction editor
Jennifer Metsker, marketing assistant